First published by Hodder Wayland
338 Euston Road, London NW1 3BH, United Kingdom
Hodder Wayland is an imprint of Hodder Children's
Books, a division of Hodder Headline Limited.
This edition published under license from Hodder
Children's Books. All rights reserved.

Text copyright © 2002 Sam Godwin
Illustrations copyright © 2002 Simone Abel
Volume copyright © 2002 Hodder Wayland

Series concept and design by Liz Black
Book design by Jane Hawkins
Edited by Katie Orchard
Science consultant: Dr. Carol Ballard

Published in the United States by
Smart Apple Media
1980 Lookout Drive
North Mankato, Minnesota 56003

U.S. publication copyright © 2003 Smart Apple Media
International copyright reserved in all countries. No part
of this book may be reproduced in any form without
written permission from the publisher.
Printed and bound in Grafiasa, Portugal

Library of Congress Cataloging-in-Publication Data

Godwin, Sam.
  Which switch is which? / by Sam Godwin. p. cm. – (Little bees)
  Summary: Illustrations and simple text describe how electricity is car-
  ried around a home and turned on by switches.
  1. Electric switchgear – Juvenile literature.
  2. Electricity – Juvenile literature. [1. Electricity.]
  I. Title.
  II. Series.

    ISBN 1-58340-224-1

    TK2831 .G57 2002   621.319'24 – dc21   2002023135

    9 8 7 6 5 4 3 2 1

Which Switch is Which?

A first look at electricity

Which Switch is Which?
A first look at electricity

Sam Godwin

A⁺

Smart Apple Media

It is nighttime. All is quiet and still.

Come on, let's find something to eat.

6

7

So we turn on the lights.

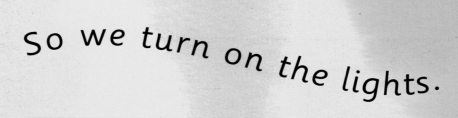

Electricity comes from a power station.

It flows along wires and into our homes.

So, the wires must come in through a hole in the wall!

14

And more wires carry the electricity

That silly moth keeps flying towards the light.

from the switches to the lights.

19

Electricity not only gives us light.

Yuck!

It makes things move...

What's this, Mommy?

It's a plug. Plugs connect things to the switches.

This washing machine uses electricity, too.

21

23

...it keeps things cold...

24

29

All about electricity

When it's dark, we need electric light to be able to see clearly.

Electricity travels into our homes along wires. The wires are connected to switches around the home.

Flipping a switch turns a light on.

Flipping a switch turns a light off.

Electricity makes lots of things work around the home.

It can make things hot or cold.

It can make sound.

And it can make things move.

Useful Words

Plug
This connects electrical objects to switches.

Power station
A place where electricity is made.

Shock
Electricity can pass through people and give them a nasty shock.

Switch
This can turn on or off the supply of electricity to an object.

Important
Electricity can be dangerous:

- Always ask an adult to help you turn on switches.
- Never touch any switches or plugs with wet hands.
- Never play with electric objects.